Children of the World

thanassis

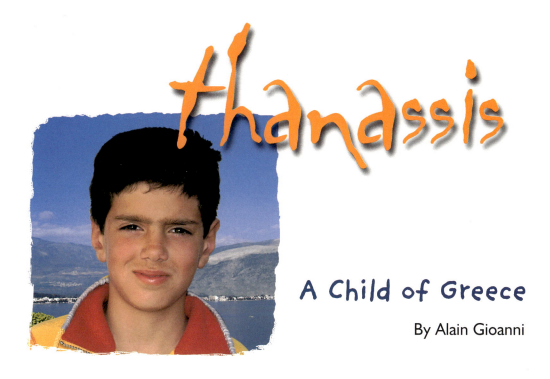

A Child of Greece

By Alain Gioanni

BLACKBIRCH PRESS
An imprint of Thomson Gale, a part of The Thomson Corporation

Detroit • New York • San Francisco • San Diego • New Haven, Conn. • Waterville, Maine • London • Munich

© Éditions PEMF, 2000

First published by PEMF in France as *Thanassis, enfant de Gréce.*

First published in North America in 2005 by Thomson Gale.

Thomson and Star Logo are trademarks and Gale and Blackbirch Press are registered trademarks used herein under license.

For more information, contact
Blackbirch Press
27500 Drake Rd.
Farmington Hills, MI 48331-3535
Or you can visit our Internet site at http://www.gale.com

ALL RIGHTS RESERVED.
No part of this work covered by the copyright hereon may be reproduced or used in any form or by any means—graphic, electronic, or mechanical, including photocopying, recording, taping, Web distribution or information storage retrieval systems—without the written permission of the publisher.

Every effort has been made to trace the owners of copyrighted material.

Photo Credits: All photos © Alain Gioanni except pages 10 (large), 11 (all), 19 (bottom), 20 (left), 22 (bottom) © Corel Corporation; Table of Contents collage: EXPLORER/Boutin (upper left); François Goalec (upper middle and right); Muriel Nicolotti (bottom left); CIRIC/Michel Gauvry (bottom middle); CIRIC/Pascal Deloche (bottom right)

LIBRARY OF CONGRESS CATALOGING-IN-PUBLICATION DATA

Gioanni, Alain.
 Thanassis : a child of Greece / by Alain Gioanni.
   p. cm. — (Children of the world)
   ISBN 1-4103-0284-9 (hard cover : alk. paper)
 1. Greece—Social life and customs—Juvenile literature. 2. Children—Greece—Social life and customs—Juvenile literature. I. Title. II. Series: Children of the world (Blackbirch Press)

DF741.G63 2005
949.507'6—dc22

2005000704

Printed in the United States of America
10 9 8 7 6 5 4 3 2 1

Contents

Facts About Greece 5
Discovering Greece 6
Thanassis, Child of Delphi 8
Ancient Delphi 10
Thanassis at School 12
Getting to Andros 14
Animal Raising 16
Fishing 17
Agriculture 18
Food 20
Ancient Greece 22
Other Books in the Series 24

Facts About Greece

Agriculture:	olive oil, cotton, wine, citrus, wheat, barley, corn, tomatoes, tobacco, animal raising
Capital:	Athens
Government:	parliamentary democracy since 1975
Industry:	food processing, textiles, boat and ship building, marine shipping
Land Area:	50,942 square miles (131,957 square kilometers)
Language:	Greek
Money:	the drachma
Natural Resources:	tourism, food and tobacco processing, textiles, chemicals, metal products, mining, oil
Population:	10,976,000
Religion:	Orthodox Christianity (98%), the state religion until 1981; Islam (1.3%); Catholicism (0.7%)

Discovering Greece

Greece is located at the far end of the Balkan peninsula. The country spreads out over the 437 islands of the Ionian Sea and the Aegean Sea.

Inset: The Meteors are monasteries built by monks and hermits on rocky peaks.

Below: The city of Athens, the capital of Greece.

Left: Many villages in Greece are located next to the sea.

Below: Heavy snowfalls occur in the mountains.

Greece is the birthplace of mythology. Its monuments, which attract many visitors each year, show off the richness of its history.

Controlled for a long time by Turkey, Greece won independence in 1924 at the end of a long war. Since 1981, it has been part of the European Economic Community (EEC).

Thanassis, Child of Delphi

Thanassis lives in Delphi, a little village perched above the sea. He has a brother, Kostas, and two sisters, Stavroula and Anna.

Inset: Thanassis and his brother and sisters.

Below: A Greek Orthodox chapel in the midst of olive trees.

Above: The village of Delphi.

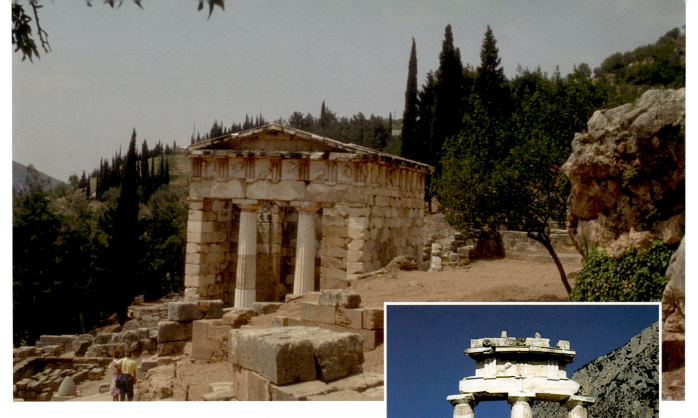

Ancient Delphi

Long ago, Delphi was a sacred city. People came from all over Greece, carrying rich presents for

Right: The ancient part of Delphi is renowned for its archaeological sites.

Apollo, the god of light. Thanassis's father works in the archaeological museum of Delphi.

Right: Charioteer statue in the Delphi Museum.

Below: The Temple of Apollo at Delphi.

Thanassis at School

Thanassis is a student at the primary school, which is called demotiko. He is learning to read and write Greek. After school, he does his homework with his brother and big sister.

Above: Thanassis and his siblings study at the kitchen table.

Right: Thanassis at the entrance to his school.

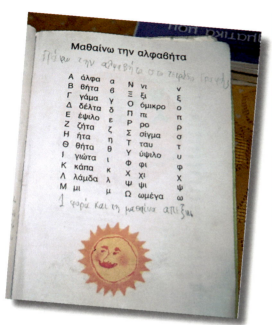

The Greek alphabet.

The Greek alphabet is different from the English alphabet. The letters are not A, B, C, D, and so on. They are alpha, beta, gamma, delta, and so on.

Getting to Andros

The boat taxi that takes Thanassis to Andros.

Below: A traditional pigeon coop on the island of Andros.

To get to the island of Andros, Thanassis must take a boat taxi. It is a boat that transports trucks full of sheep as well as tourist buses.

Among the many islands of Greece, Andros is part of the 39 that make up the archipelago of the Cyclades. These islands are exposed to sun and wind. The houses are painted white and blue.

Above: The port of Gavrion, as the boat taxi approaches.

Left: Night has fallen. The island sleeps peacefully.

Animal Raising

Thanassis really likes a kind of cheese called feta. This cheese is made on farms from sheeps' milk.

Even if raising animals is not the main farming activity, it is a tradition. It is not uncommon to see shepherds seated on their donkeys, watching over their flocks of sheep and goats. The wool from these animals is used to make rugs.

Above: A shepherd watches over his flock of sheep.

Below: Cheese making in the village of Arachova. This kind of cheese is eaten fried.

Fishing

Below: Fishermen repair their nets.

Thanassis enjoys talking to the fishermen who, after a day at sea, sit and repair their nets.

Fishing is common in a country where the sea is no farther than 50 miles (80 kilometers) away from any point. Many people make a living fishing, and the tourists enjoy it too.

Agriculture

This farm, like all farms in the mountains, is terraced.

The mountainous terrain in Greece makes farming difficult. The farmers have to terrace the land in order to plant and harvest crops.

Below: Olive trees are an important natural resource in Greece.

Above: The olive groves of Delphi.

The Mediterranean climate is ideal for olive trees, which are a source of wealth for the country. The olive groves around Delphi, for example, have more than 9 million trees!

Food

Greek cuisine is typically Mediterranean and based on local products. Thanassis likes olives and olive oil.

Olives, the fruit of the olive tree.

Thanassis also likes tzatziki (Greek yogurt with grated cucumber and garlic), slouvakias (shish kebab), and moussaka (a baked dish of meat and eggplant).

Tzatziki

Ancient Greece

The monuments of ancient Greece were built in honor of the Greek gods. They are proof of the richness of past civilizations. They have been preserved over centuries. They are one of the big tourist attractions of Greece.

Above: The ancient stadium in Delphi, where the Pythian Games were played.

Below: The Parthenon in Athens.

Pollution and earthquakes are constant threats to these ancient sites.

Left: A house damaged by the earthquake of September 7, 1999.

Right: A cloud of pollution blankets the city of Athens.

23

Other Books in the Series

Arafat: A Child of Tunisia
Asha: A Child of the Himalayas
Avinesh: A Child of the Ganges
Ballel: A Child of Senegal
Basha: A Hmong Child
Frederico: A Child of Brazil

Ituko: An Inuit Child
Kradji: A Child of Cambodia
Kuntai: A Masai Child
Leila: A Tuareg Child
Madhi: A Child of Egypt
Tomasino: A Child of Peru